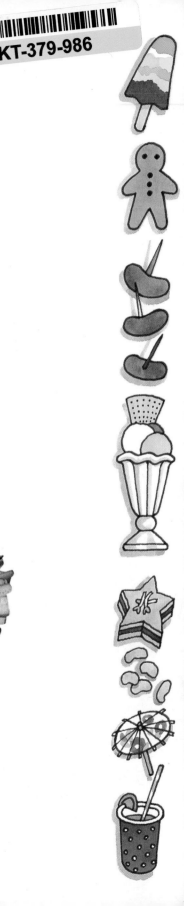

CHILDREN'S
-Party-
FOOD

Devised and illustrated by

Clare Beaton

Kingfisher Books

CONTENTS

Produced by Times Four Publishing Ltd
Art and editorial direction: Tony Potter
Copy editor: Nicola Wright
Home economist· Lycross caterers

Kingfisher Books, Grisewood & Dempsey Ltd,
Elsley House, 24-30 Great Titchfield St, London W1P 7AD

First published in 1991 by Kingfisher Books

10 9 8 7 6 5 4 3 2 1

Colour separations by RCS Graphics, Leeds
Typeset by C-Type, Horley, Surrey
Printed in Spain

BRITISH LIBRARY CATALOGUING IN PUBLICATION DATA
Beaton, Clare
    Children's party food.
    1. Entertainment. Food. Party dishes. Recipes
I. Title   II. Series
641.568

ISBN 0-86272-702-2

INTRODUCTION

The best party food is fun and easy to eat. Keep ideas simple and colourful. If you are having a party with a theme, you could make some of the food to match.

Sandwiches, biscuits, jelly and ice cream are always popular at any party tea. With the main components for a party tea in mind, this book has been divided into sections, each giving lots of novel but simple ideas for you to choose from.

Much of the food can be cooked or prepared in advance, and kept in the freezer or airtight containers. Cakes and biscuits can be iced and decorated the morning before the party.

Many children get too excited at parties to eat large amounts, so don't overdo the quantities. Bite-size 'nibbles' usually go down well with children as they can try a bit of everything.

It's a good idea to have a variety of savoury and sweet things on the table to cater for different tastes. Food cut or arranged in novel shapes will appeal most to children.

It's also a good idea to set individual places at the tea table for each guest. Provide plenty of colourful napkins, as most of the party food will be eaten with their fingers.

Colour is perhaps the most important thing to consider when preparing a party tea. Bright colours always look good, but avoid using too many lurid or dark colours as these will look less appetising.

Natural food colourings are available such as beetroot red, annatto, anthracene, riboflavin and cochineal. When shopping, check ingredients carefully to avoid too many E numbers in the form of artificial colours, preservatives and sweeteners.

Other ingredients to avoid include whole nuts and anything that could get stuck in children's throats. Also beware of serving strong tasting or spicy food to children. It's safer to make simple dishes, then concentrate on decorating and presenting them attractively.

TABLE DECOR

The food table is usually the central attraction of the party, so decorate it with special care. If you are having a party with a theme, it adds to the fun to try and match the table decor and some of the food to it. For example, at a space party you could cover the table and plates with silver foil and dangle cardboard planets and moons from a string strung above the table. However you decide to decorate your table, make sure it is well covered with spillproof material, and always provide plenty of paper napkins.

Place mats

Novelty-shaped individual place mats can be cut out of cardboard or thick paper. Simply use a stencil or tracing, or draw round an appropriate object. Make large circles for a spotty party, or top hats for a circus party and get the children to colour and decorate their own when they arrive.

Place names

To avoid any arguments over where everyone is to sit, it is a good idea to put each guest's name already at a place setting. The birthday child may enjoy writing these on folded pieces of card and perhaps drawing the person's face too. Again, if you are having a theme, you could cut the cards into appropriate shapes.

Plates and cups

You can buy many different kinds of patterned plastic and paper party cups and plates. However, you may prefer to decorate some yourself, with stickers or sticky stars and spots. Do not use spray paints or pens to colour anything that will come in contact with food, as they may be toxic.

Hats and masks

You could make or buy a party hat or mask for each child and have them ready to wear beside their place at the table. These could match your theme if you're having one. Children also love having party blowers and streamers to play with at the table.

Finishing touches

Put bendy straws and paper umbrellas in drinks for a fun touch. Place bite-size pieces of food on cocktail sticks and stick into half grapefruits or oranges for a 'hedgehog' effect. When you are ready for the cake, dim the lights and make a grand entrance with candles alight.

SANDWICHES

Children find sandwiches made from thinly sliced bread easier to eat. Make a variety of different fillings, clearly marked.

Make the sandwiches on the day of the party, keeping them well covered so they don't dry out. Garnish them at the last minute with mustard and cress or twists of cucumber.

There are plenty of novel ways you can serve sandwiches to make them more appealing. Try cutting them into different shapes using biscuit cutters.

SANDWICH WHEELS

Cut the crusts off slices of brown bread. Then, with a rolling pin, roll the slices out lightly and spread thickly with cream cheese. Place a stick of celery across one end of each slice and roll up tightly. Wrap the rolls in foil until just before eating. Then cut them into 10mm (½ in) slices to serve.

CHESSBOARD

Arrange small squares of brown and white sandwiches like a chessboard.

CROISSANTS

Croissants can be stuffed with sweet or savoury fillings. You could also use bagels and differently flavoured breads. Look out for bakeries or delicatessens selling animal-shaped rolls and loaves.

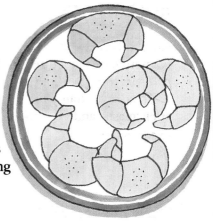

OPEN SANDWICHES

Open sandwiches can be endlessly varied and look very colourful and attractive. Don't overload the bread or the topping will fall off.

Marmite and cheese

Cress

Radish

Cream cheese

Carrot

Olive

Slice of cucumber

Shaped cheese slice on cream cheese

Round slices of cold meat

Beetroot

Cucumber

ROLL BOATS

Slice rolls or small baguettes in half, butter and spread with filling. Then add cocktail stick 'masts' and paper 'sails'.

LABELS

Cut out appropriate shapes from paper as labels to stick into plates of sandwiches using cocktail sticks.

SANDWICH HOUSE

A sandwich house is simple to construct and makes a fun centrepiece on the table. Cut square sandwiches for the main building, arranging them in a solid block as big as you like but not higher than three sandwiches or they will fall over. Cut triangular sandwiches for the roof, buttering both sides of the bread to help stick the sandwiches together (cocktail sticks can also be used to help secure the sandwiches). Cut vegetables for windows, doors etc.

Twiglets or cheese straws for roof

Carrot Windows

Carrot door

SMALL CAKES

Bake lots of small sponge cakes. You can freeze them if you want to make them in advance.

SPONGE MIXTURE

To make about 16 fairy cakes you will need...

150g or 6oz softened
    butter or margarine
150g or 6oz caster
    sugar
3 eggs
150g or 6oz self-
    raising flour

Set the oven at 180°C/350°F/Gas Mark 4. Put the softened butter and sugar in a mixing bowl and beat with a wooden spoon until the mixture is pale and creamy. Beat the eggs separately, then add them to the butter and sugar mixture a little at a time, stirring well until smooth. Sift the flour into the mixture and mix well.

Spoon the mixture into individual paper cases and smooth level. Bake the cakes in the oven for 15-20 minutes until risen and golden brown.

CHOCOLATE CRISPIES

Chocolate crispies are popular with children, both to make and eat. They are very easy to make as no baking is required.

Simply melt some chocolate in a bowl, then stir in Cornflakes or Rice Krispies. Place large spoonfuls in cake cases and allow to cool and harden.

GLACÉ ICING

Glacé icing is easy to make and can be used to decorate cakes and biscuits. Sift icing sugar into a bowl. Add hot water a little at a time, mixing it with the sugar to make a smooth paste.

Use a wet knife to help spread it. You can add food colouring to glacé icing, or make a chocolate variation by replacing a quarter of the icing sugar with cocoa powder.

Colour glacé icing
with food colourings.

BUTTERFLY CAKES

Make the fairy cakes as usual. Then, when cool, carefully cut a shallow hole out of the top of each. Fill the hole with butter icing. To make the butterfly wings slice the cut-off top piece in two and stick the straight edges together into the icing at an angle.

Butter
icing

Wings

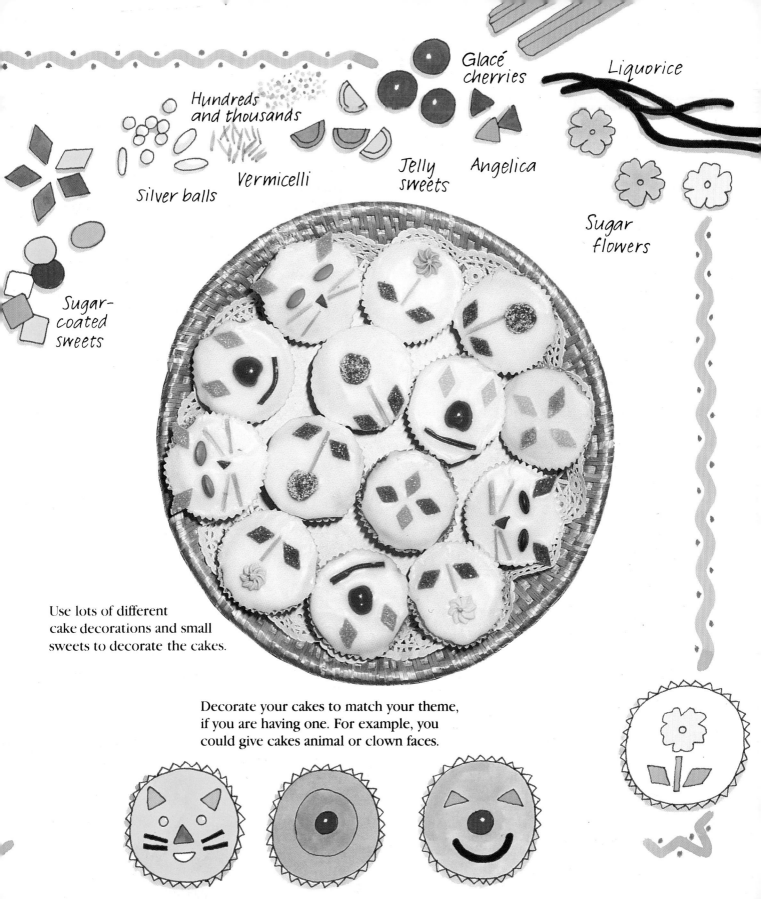

Hundreds
and thousands

Silver balls

Vermicelli

Jelly
sweets

Glacé
cherries

Angelica

Liquorice

Sugar
flowers

Sugar-
coated
sweets

Use lots of different
cake decorations and small
sweets to decorate the cakes.

Decorate your cakes to match your theme,
if you are having one. For example, you
could give cakes animal or clown faces.

JELLIES

Individual jellies in paper dishes are pretty. Make several different flavours. You can add a little chopped up fruit at the bottom and a blob of 'spray' cream on top.

A large jelly made in a mould makes an amusing centrepiece, though looks rather messy once cut.

Pink rabbit with 'mashed' green jelly around it on a plate.

MILK JELLIES

Melt jelly in hot water as normal, then top up to required amount with fresh or evaporated milk. For a striped effect, make half the jelly with water, leave it to set, then add a layer of milk jelly.

MAGIC JELLIES

You will need...

Large oranges
Packets of differently flavoured jelly

Cut the oranges in two and carefully scoop all the flesh out of the halves. Stand the empty skins on trays (use bits of Plasticine to help keep them upright).

Use bits of Plasticine or Blu-tack to hold up the fruit.

Use differently coloured jellies.

Then make up the jellies. Don't use quite so much water as instructed on the packet to ensure the jelly sets firmly. Pour the jelly into the orange skins up to the top. When set, carefully cut each orange half into three 'segments'.

The segments 'magically' have jelly inside the real orange skin. It's fun to make lots of different colours.

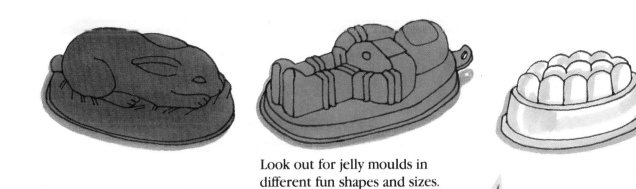

Look out for jelly moulds in different fun shapes and sizes.

Make jelly 'boats' using cocktail sticks and paper 'sails'.

Sea of mashed-up blue jelly

STRIPED JELLY

Set different coloured layers of jelly in glasses for a striped effect. Allow each new layer to set before adding the next colour.

JELLY KEBABS

Set differently coloured jellies in ice cube trays with the divider removed (or in a shallow plastic tray). Use slightly less liquid than instructed on the packet. Then cut the jelly into cubes and thread on to skewers.

DRINKS

If you want to be more adventurous with drinks than the basic juices, squashes and fizzy drinks, here are some simple recipes to try:

MILKSHAKES

You will need...

325g or 12oz fresh
   fruit
2 tablespoons caster
   sugar
900ml or 1½ pints milk
4 scoops vanilla ice
   cream

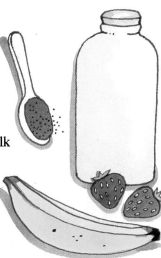

Place half the fruit, sugar, milk and ice cream in an electric blender or food processor. Blend for 20 seconds, then pour into a jug. Repeat with the remaining ingredients. This recipe makes 1.2 litres (2 pints) of natural, creamy milkshake. Serve in tall glasses with straws.

ICE CREAM SODAS

Fill glasses half full with lemonade, then add scoops of ice cream. You could use cola or cherryade instead.

FRUIT PUNCH

Top glasses of fruit juice up with lemonade. In the winter you could make a hot punch with blackcurrant drink, orange juice and water.

HOT CHOCOLATE

Marshmallows floating in hot chocolate make a delicious treat in the winter. Alternatively, spray cream on top of a hot chocolate drink and grate chocolate on top, or sprinkle on hundreds and thousands. Serve with teaspoons.

Cream

Marshmallows

HOMEMADE LEMONADE

For a refreshing and natural lemonade try this quick and easy recipe:

You will need...

4 lemons
75g or 3oz caster
   sugar
1.2 litres or 2 pints
   boiling water

Grate the rind from the lemons and place in a heatproof jug with the sugar. Pour over the water and stir until the sugar has dissolved. Squeeze the lemons and strain into the jug. Allow to cool. Makes 1.2 litres (2 pints).

MAGIC POTION

For a very fizzy effect, freeze chocolate drops and place a few at the bottom of each glass. Then fill the glasses with sparkling drink.

Put slices of orange and lemon on the rim of glasses.

Dip the rims of glasses in lemon juice, then sugar or coconut.

Make decorations for straws. Keep them simple and place near the top of the straw.

Tissue flowers

Butterfly

Names

Cleo

Tinsel

Paper fruit

Bat

Spider

13

PIZZAS

You can make pizza bases well in advance and freeze them. When ready to cook, cover the bases in a tomato sauce (see recipe below). All the additional toppings can be selected and added by the children at the party. Let them do this between games so the pizzas can be ready to eat from the oven when the meal starts.

PIZZA DOUGH

This recipe makes two 10cm (4 in) pizza bases.

You will need....

150g or 6oz self-
   raising flour
Pinch of salt and
   pepper
40g or 1½ oz butter or
   margarine
50g or 2oz grated cheese
3-4 tablespoons milk

Chop up the butter and place in a bowl with the flour and seasoning. Rub in the butter until the mixture looks like breadcrumbs. Add the grated cheese and the milk and mix it all together until you have a small ball of dough. Divide the dough in half and roll out into 10cm (4 in) circles. Once the pizza bases have been covered with tomato sauce and toppings, bake them for 15-20 minutes at 220°C/425°F/Gas Mark 7 until the edges are golden brown.

Have the bases already on baking trays if the children are going to decorate their own. To prevent the pizzas getting muddled up, you could get the children to make distinguishing marks in their decoration, or write their names on strips of greaseproof paper tucked under the bases.

PIZZA SAUCE

You will need...

1 small onion
1 small tin tomatoes
1 dessertspoon tomato
   pureé
Pinch of salt and
   pepper

Break up the tinned tomatoes with a fork and mix in the tomato pureé, (or put into a blender or food processor for a few seconds). Heat the mixture together with the chopped onion and seasoning for 15 minutes in a saucepan. Allow the sauce to cool before spreading on the pizza bases.

MINI PIZZAS

Crumpets or muffins can be used as bases for mini pizzas. Add tomato sauce and toppings in the normal way.

Individual mini quiches would also go down well. Bake them in pretty frilled pastry cases.

Names on greaseproof paper

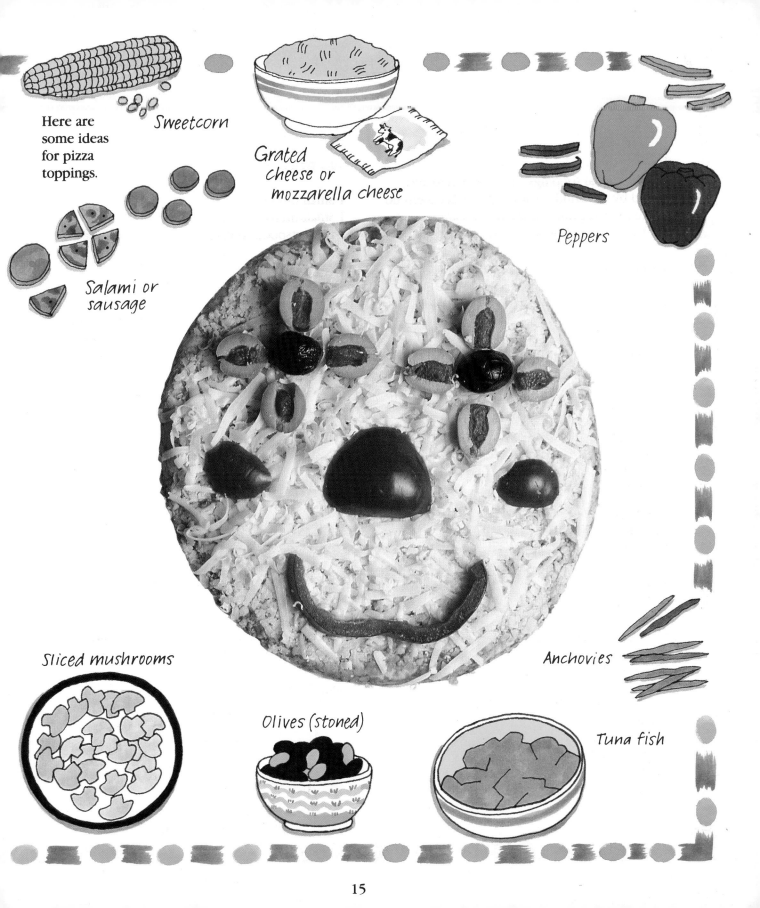

Here are some ideas for pizza toppings.

Sweetcorn

Grated cheese or mozzarella cheese

Peppers

Salami or sausage

Sliced mushrooms

Olives (stoned)

Anchovies

Tuna fish

15

FRUIT

Most children love fresh fruit. What you choose to serve obviously depends on the season. Tinned or frozen fruit can also be used. Many fruits are now tinned in their natural juice rather than syrup, and these are healthier.

FRUIT KEBABS

Dip small fruits, such as strawberries, grapes or tangerine segments, half way into melted chocolate. Leave them until the chocolate has hardened, then thread on to cocktail sticks to serve.

BANANAS

Bananas are especially popular with children. For a special treat, dip whole bananas in melted chocolate and then roll them in hundreds and thousands.

You can also bake bananas in their skins, either in the oven or in the embers of a bonfire, until the skins are blackened. Peel back a strip of skin when cool enough to eat and serve on a plate with cream and brown sugar.

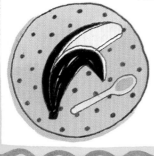

Make sure the bananas are cool enough to serve.

TOFFEE APPLES

You will need...

14 short wooden sticks
14 medium dessert
    apples
675g or 1lb demerara
    sugar
75g or 3oz butter or
    margarine
2 teaspoons vinegar
175ml or 6fl oz water
2 tablespoons golden
    syrup

Push a stick firmly into the core of each apple. Heat the other ingredients gently in a large heavy-based saucepan until the sugar has dissolved. Bring to the boil and boil for 5 minutes, without stirring, until 143°C (290°F) is reached on a sugar thermometer, or until a little mixture dropped into cold water goes hard. Remove from the heat and stand in cold water to stop the mixture cooking.

You could wrap the apples in paper.

Dip the apples one at a time into the mixture. Lift each apple out and twirl over the pan until evenly coated with toffee. Place on an oiled baking sheet until the toffee has hardened.

FRUIT SALAD

Cut the top off a pineapple and carefully scoop out the flesh. Cut the flesh into cubes and mix it with other fruit. Fill the pineapple with the fruit. Keep in the fridge until ready to serve.

You could use a melon instead of a pineapple.

Pour a little orange juice over the fruit salad.

Lemon juice stops fruit going brown.

Cut large fruit into cubes or use whole small fruits. Put on to cocktail sticks and push into half a grapefruit or a large orange.

BARBECUE

Barbecues are fun either for lunchtime or a summer tea, or in the winter as part of a firework party. If you don't want to cook a lot, even hot dogs and warmed pitta bread will make a nice change and are easy to do. Afterwards the children can toast marshmallows. Remember always to have an adult in charge of the barbecue to avoid any accidents.

KEBABS

Cut chicken and pork into cubes and thread alternately on to metal skewers. For extra flavour, marinate the meat for several hours before cooking (see the recipe opposite).

Add vegetables such as cherry tomatoes, pickled onions and chunks of pepper for a bit of colour.

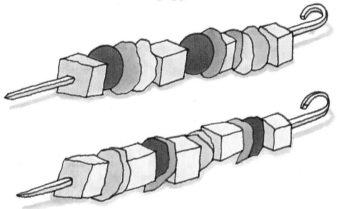

JACKET POTATOES

Cut baked potatoes in half and scoop out the insides. Mash them together with grated cheese and butter or margarine and spoon back into the skins. Garnish with cress, or use cocktail sticks and slices of cheese and pepper to make 'boats'.

MARINADE

HONEY AND ORANGE

You will need...

2 tablespoons clear honey
1 tablespoon Worcester sauce
Grated rind and juice of ½ orange
1 tablespoon tomato pureé
1 tablespoon soy sauce

Mix all the ingredients together in a bowl and brush over chicken drumsticks or any meat. Cover the meat completely in silver foil and marinate for at least 1 hour before cooking. Use any remaining sauce to baste the meat while it is on the barbecue.

PITTAS

Mini 'party' pittas are a good alternative to the normal burger buns as small children will find them fun and easier to eat. Warm them up in the oven first, then slit open one end and fill with salad, pieces of hamburger or vegiburger and slices of cheese. Serve with a paper napkin.

A BARBECUE CAFÉ

Write a menu on a blackboard or piece of card
and serve your guests from a table.

Mini filled pittas,
ready to serve.

'PIG IN A BLANKET'

A 'pig in a blanket' is an original way to barbecue
sausages or frankfurters. Wrap a couple of rashers
of bacon around each sausage, leaving the ends
sticking out. Use cocktail sticks to secure the
ends. Cook over the barbecue.

Chestnuts are good to
roast at the end of a
winter barbecue. Eat
them with salt and
butter.

BISCUITS

Biscuits are very popular and easy to make. A tray of these in different shapes, iced and brightly decorated, is ideal for children to take into school on their birthday.

BUTTER BISCUITS

To make 20 biscuits
you will need...

100g or 4oz butter or
  margarine
100g or 4oz caster
  sugar
1 egg
225g or 8oz plain flour
Rind from 1 lemon,
  finely grated

Set the oven at 180°C/350°F/Gas Mark 4. Cream the butter and caster sugar together until light and fluffy. Then beat in the egg gradually. Stir in the seived flour and lemon rind to form a stiff dough. Knead the dough lightly and roll out to 5mm (¼ in) thick. Cut into required shapes and place on lightly greased baking trays. Bake until a light golden colour. When cooked, place the biscuits on a wire rack to cool.

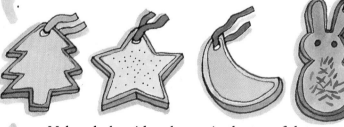

Make a hole with a skewer in the top of the biscuits before cooking. When cooked and allowed to cool, thread with ribbon or wool and hang up or give out as going home presents.

SPICY BISCUITS

To make 24 biscuits
you will need...

275g or 10oz self-
  raising flour
1 dessertspoon of
  cinnamon
100g or 4oz soft brown
  sugar
75g or 3oz butter or
  margarine
1 small egg
50g or 2oz golden
  syrup

Set the oven at 170°C/325°F/Gas Mark 3. Sift the flour and cinnamon into a mixing bowl, then stir in the sugar, Cut up the butter and rub it into the mixture until it looks like breadcrumbs. Beat the egg separately with a fork and then add the golden syrup to it, mixing until smooth. Make a hollow in the flour mixture and pour in the egg mixture. Mix together until you have a big ball of dough. Place the dough in a plastic bag and keep in the fridge for 30 minutes. Roll out, cut, and bake as with butter biscuits.

Children will love to help cut out the biscuits in different shapes and decorating them by pressing chopped nuts, currants or sesame seeds into the dough. When cooked you can decorate with icing, cake decorations and sweets.

Using the spicy biscuits recipe, make gingerbread people and write the guests' name on them, using tubes of icing.

You could dip some biscuits half into melted chocolate.

Decorate the biscuits with jellies and sweets.

Arrange lots of different biscuits on a plate.

Make biscuits to match the theme of your party.

ICE CREAM

Most children enjoy ice cream. Whether you make your own or buy it, serving ice cream with a sauce makes it extra special for a party. These sauce recipes can be made a few days in advance and kept in the fridge.

BUTTERSCOTCH SAUCE

You will need...

284ml or 10fl oz carton
   double cream
100g or 4oz unsalted
   butter
150g or 6oz soft
   brown sugar

Place all the ingredients in a heavy-based saucepan. Heat gently, stirring until the sugar has dissolved. Then bring to the boil and boil for 2 minutes, until syrupy. Serve hot or cold.

MAKING SUNDAES

Put various flavours of ice cream, the sauces and as many toppings as you like out on a table so the the children can construct their own sundae. Try to avoid a mad scramble all at once, and have the table and surrounding area well covered! Alternatively, put single scoops of ice cream in ramekins or small bowls and decorate as faces or animals.

CHOCOLATE SAUCE

You will need...

150g or 6oz plain
   chocolate, chopped
50g or 2oz caster
   sugar
250ml or 8fl oz milk

Place all the ingredients in a saucepan and heat gently, stirring until the sugar has dissolved. Simmer for 2 to 3 minutes. Serve hot or cold.

RASPBERRY SAUCE

You will need...

150g or 6oz raspberries,
   frozen or fresh
75g or 3oz caster sugar

Wash the raspberries and push them through a sieve over a bowl using a wooden spoon. Add the caster sugar to the raspberry pulp a little at a time. Then stir the sauce vigorously until all the sugar has dissolved. Serve hot or cold.

MARS BAR SAUCE

For a very quick and delicious sauce, gently melt Mars bars in a saucepan with a little milk.

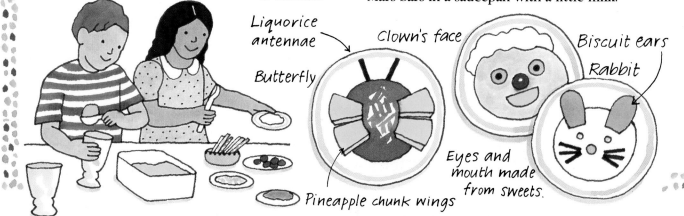

Liquorice antennae

Butterfly

Pineapple chunk wings

Clown's face

Biscuit ears

Rabbit

Eyes and mouth made from sweets.

Add a miniature umbrella for a final, fun touch.

Put all the toppings into small bowls or saucers with a spoon in each.

Chopped fruit, fresh or tinned

Vermicelli

Chocolate logs

Glacé cherries

'Spray' Cream is the easiest to use.

Cream

Hundreds and thousands

Chocolate drops

Chopped nuts

Wafers

Sponge fingers

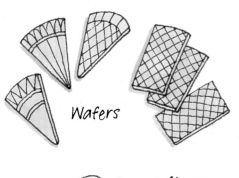

Use thick glasses or glass sweet dishes if you can't get sundae glasses.

SALADS

Children can be very fussy about eating salad and fresh vegetables, so take extra care to present vegetables in a novel and attractive way. Make use of the naturally colourful varieties for decoration.

VEGETABLE SHAPES

Cut brightly coloured vegetables, such as peppers, carrots and tomatoes, into shapes and use to garnish plates of sandwiches. You could also thread chunks on to cocktail sticks to make vegetable kebabs.

VEGETABLE KEBABS

Vegetable shapes and small vegetables such as radishes look good threaded alternately on to skewers.

TOMATOES

Scoop the insides out of cherry tomatoes and fill them with cream cheese. You can have fun arranging the tomatoes in amusing and interesting patterns, for example the age of the birthday child.

VEGETABLE DIP

Slice carrots, cucumbers, courgettes, and celery sticks into small, thin strips and serve with a dip. Avoid any strong or spicy ingredients. Try mixing cream cheese or peanut butter with yogurt, or tomato ketchup and salad cream or mayonnaise.

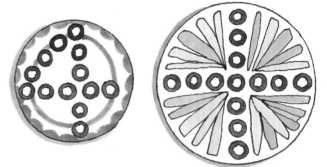